D0836364

Ranma 1/2™

VOL. 8 **Action Edition**

STORY & ART BY

RUMIKO TAKAHASHI

RANMA 1/2

VOL. 8
Action Edition

Story and Art by
RUMIKO TAKAHASHI

English Adaptation by Gerard Jones & Toshifumi Yoshida
Touch-Up Art & Lettering/Wayne Truman
Cover and Interior Design & Graphics/Yuki Ameda
Editor (1st Edition)/Trish Ledoux
Editor (Action Edition)/Julie Davis

Managing Editor/Annette Roman
Editorial Director/Alvin Lu
Director of Production/Noboru Watanabe
Sr. Dir. of Licensing & Acquisitions/Rika Inouye
V.P. of Sales & Marketing/Liza Coppola
Executive V.P./Hyoe Narita
Publisher/Seiji Horibuchi

RANMA 1/2 is rated "T+" for Older Teens. It may contain violence, language, alcohol or tobacco use, or suggestive situations.

The stories, characters and incidents mentioned in this publication are entirely fictional. For the purposes of publication in English, the artwork in this publication is printed in reverse from the original Japanese version.

Printed in Canada.

Published by VIZ, LLC
P.O. Box 77010
San Francisco, CA 94107

1st Edition published 1997

Action Edition
10 9 8 7 6 5 4 3 2
First printing, January 2004
Second printing, October 2004

VIZ
www.viz.com

STORY THUS FAR

The Tendos are an average, run-of-the-mill Japanese family—at least on the surface, that is. Soun Tendo is the owner and proprietor of the Tendo Dojo, where "Anything-Goes Martial Arts" is practiced. Like the name says, anything goes, and usually does.

When Soun's old friend Genma Saotome comes to visit, Soun's three lovely young daughters—Akane, Nabiki, and Kasumi—are told that it's time for one of them to become the fiancée of Genma's teenage son, as per an agreement made between the two fathers years ago. Youngest daughter Akane—who says she hates boys—is quickly nominated for bridal duty by her sisters.

Unfortunately, Ranma and his father have suffered a strange accident. While training in China, both plunged into one of many "accursed" springs at the legendary martial arts training ground of Jusenkyo. These springs transform the unlucky dunkee into whoever—or whatever—drowned there hundreds of years ago.

From now on, a splash of cold water turns Ranma's father into a giant panda, and Ranma becomes a beautiful, busty young woman. Hot water reverses the effect...but only until next time.

Ranma and Genma weren't the only ones to take the Jusenkyo plunge—it isn't long before they meet several other members of the "cursed." And although their parents are still determined to see Ranma and Akane marry and carry on the training hall, Ranma seems to have a strange talent for accumulating extra fiancées, and Akane has a few suitors of her own. Will the two ever work out their differences, get rid of all these extra people, or just call the whole thing off? And will Ranma ever get rid of his curse?

CAST OF CHARACTERS

RANMA SAOTOME
Martial artist with far too many fiancées, and an ego that won't let him take defeat easily. He changes into a girl when splashed with cold water.

SHAMPOO
A Chinese Amazon warrior who has changed her mind from wanting to kill Ranma to wanting to marry him.

RYOGA HIBIKI
A melancholy martial artist with no sense of direction, a crush on Akane, and a grudge against Ranma. He changes into a small, black pig Akane calls "P-chan."

GENMA SAOTOME
Ranma's lazy father, who left his home and wife years ago with his young son to train in the martial arts. He changes into a panda.

MOUSSE
A nearsighted martial artist and Shampoo's childhood suitor, Mousse's specialty is the art of hidden weapons.

AKANE TENDO
A martial artist, tomboy, and Ranma's fiancée by parental arrangement. She has no clue how much Ryoga likes her, or what relation he has to her pet black pig, P-chan.

COLOGNE
Shampoo's great-grandmother, a martial artist and matchmaker.

HAPPOSAI
The martial arts master who trained both Genma and Soun. Also a world-class pervert.

SOUN TENDO
The head of the Tendo household and owner of the Tendo Dojo.

UKYO KUONJI
A friend of Ranma's from childhood with a flair for cooking and a grudge to settle.

CONTENTS

Part 1

"OKONOMIYAKI" MEANS "I LOVE YOU"

RRRRUUUUMM
KRA
IT'S BEEN A LONG TIME, GENMA SAOTOME.
HMM...?
HAVE WE MET BEFORE?
DON'T PRETEND THAT YOU DON'T KNOW ME...
OKONOMIYAKI
...UKYO!? THE ONE YOU LEFT BEHIND!?
VSSH
U... UKYO!?

WOW... POP GOT A LETTER OF CHALLENGE ?
TENDO TRAINING HALL
YES, AND A VERY STRANGE ONE AT THAT...

SEE ?
meet me at the empty lot at 4 o'clock
A...A CHALLENGE...
...ON OKONOMIYAKI !?

KLAKKETA
KLAKKETA

POP!

HUH ?!
TP.
FZZZZ
SSSZZZ

HEY POP!
KONK KONK KONK

ENOUGH ALREADY!
SPLAT
SNAP OUT OF IT, POP!
WAPWAP
WAP

VZZZ
WHA--?!
TWONG
VEEN VEEN
RANMA! NEXT IT'S YOUR TURN TO PAY!

LET IT GO...
...FOR YOUR OWN GOOD.

.....
THAT OKONOMIYAKI GUY...

I KEEP THINKING WE'VE MET BEFORE...
HMM...

HEY POP, HOW COME HE BEAT YOU SO EASY? YOU'RE HIDIN' SOMETHING, AREN'T YOU!?
.....

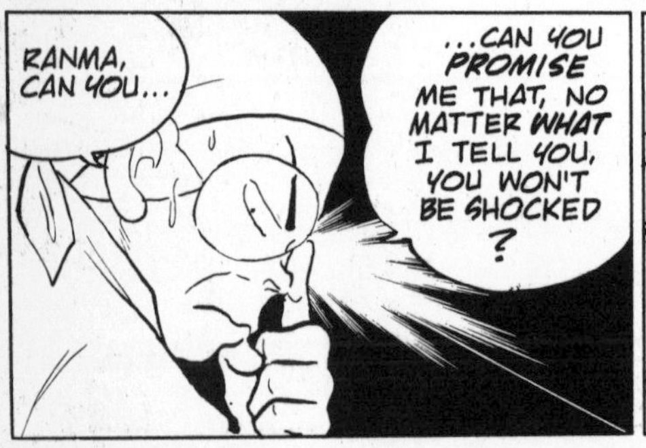
RANMA, CAN YOU...
...CAN YOU PROMISE ME THAT, NO MATTER WHAT I TELL YOU, YOU WON'T BE SHOCKED?

SURE.

THE TRUTH IS...
THEN COME CLOSER.

...THAT UKYO...

GAA!!

I WONDER IF I SHOULD TELL HIM...?
BOP
WAP
GRARARA
OOLO

I CAN'T TELL YOU...YOU'RE TOO EASILY SHOCKED...
SPLOOSH
RRING
RRING

STAY LIKE THAT FOREVER, FOR ALL I CARE!
WHP
WHP
WHP

WHAT'D YOU WANT TO TALK TO ME ABOUT, AKANE?
RANMA... UMM...

YOU'RE AN ONLY CHILD, RIGHT...?
YEAH, WHAT OF IT?

WHAT IF YOU FOUND OUT YOU... WEREN'T?
WHAT ARE YOU TALKING ABOUT?

I HAPPENED TO OVERHEAR IT...
UKYO'S CHALLENGE!

FEEL THE WRATH OF THE CHILD YOU LEFT BEHIND!
FORGIVE ME! I WAS POOR! I COULD BARELY FEED RANMA AND MYSELF!

MR. SAOTOME... HAD AN ILLEGITIMATE CHILD !?

SO THAT'S IT!

AREN'T YOU SHOCKED ?
WHO, ME ?
BONK

NAH, I DIDN'T KNOW THE OLD GUY HAD IT IN 'IM! AND WITH HIS LOOKS, TOO!

YOU PIG.
WHO SAYS I HAVE ILLEGITIMATE CHILDREN ?
OH NO? THEN WHAT WAS UKYO TALKING ABOUT?

CLASS, I'D LIKE TO INTRODUCE A NEW STUDENT...

SSSSS!
SSSSSS
SSSSSS
WH-WHAT ELEGANT TECHNIQUE.
MY HOBBY'S MAKING OKONOMIYAKI... "JAPANESE PIZZA"!
MY NAME'S UKYO KUONJI!
MURMUR
MURMUR
SSSSS
SSSSSS
HUH?
UKYO?
HEY, THAT'S--
RANMA! IT'S BEEN A LONG TIME!
SHAH
I-IT'S ALL COMIN' BACK TO ME...
AH!
PAP

YOU'RE... YOU'RE...
SHIK!
HEH.

VSSH
FOR TEN YEARS I'VE HUNTED YOU!

TA TA TAK
WAAA!
YOU'RE "UCCHAN" FROM THAT OKONOMIYAKI CART!
FLAP
POK
ERK!!

YOU WERE CHILDHOOD FRIENDS?
GASP
OHH!
YEAH! FOR A WHILE, ANYWAY.

I MET UKYO WHEN POP AND I WERE TRAINING. "UCCHAN" WAS A NICKNAME I CAME UP WITH.

UCCHAN!

TA TA TA

COMIN' FER ANOTHER FREE MEAL, EH!? LITTLE PUNK.

GET RID OF HIM, UKYO.

SSIZZZLE

KONOM

GOOD OLD UKYO...

GET READY!

THIS TIME...I WIN!

I GOT FREE OKONOMIYAKI PRACTICALLY EVERY DAY!

ISN'T THAT CALLED "THEFT"...?
NAW! TAKE A LOOK.

UKYO USED TO DRAW LITTLE PICTURES WITH THE SAUCE!
HE'D ALWAYS HAVE ONE HOT 'N' READY FOR ME.
IT WAS A SAD DAY WHEN I HAD TO GO...
A BEAUTIFUL FRIENDSHIP, BORN OF COMBAT!
WOW!
CAST YOUR MIND BACK TO THE DAY YOU LEFT.
WHAT ARE YOU SO MAD ABOUT?
HOW DARE YOU?!
BAMG
VRRRR.
BYE-BYE, UCCHAN! BYE-BYE!
WELL, LET'S SEE...
YOU WERE RUNNING AFTER US, CRYING...

VRRRRRRRRRRRRRR
YOU JERKS!
YOU SAID YOU'D TAKE ME WITH YOU!
OH? SO THEN WHAT'S WITH THE "VRRRRRR"?
THE HUH...?
BYE-BYE, UCCHAN!
JERRRRKS!
HUH!?
COME T' THINK OF IT, WHY THE HECK WERE ***WE*** TRAVELIN' ON ***YOUR*** OKONOMIYAKI CART?
AND ***THAT'S*** NOT THEFT?!
YOU'RE WRONG! UKYO'S FATHER GAVE IT TO ME!
BOOOM
MR. SAOTOME...?

WHAT IS UKYO, A LITTER OF KITTENS ?!
I WAS SUPPOSED TO TAKE UKYO AS PART OF THE DEAL, BUT ALAS...

!
YEAH, WHY WOULD YOU WANT TO COME WITH MY STUPID OLD MAN?
BUT DIDN'T YOU HAVE YOUR OWN FATHER?
MOOSH

YOU BROKE YOUR PROMISE...
...AND LEFT ME BEHIND.

RANMA...YOU REALLY DON'T KNOW?

......
PAP PAP
C'MON! BE A MAN!
WELL, WHO CARES? LET BYGONES BE BYGONES!

SO. AT LAST I UNDERSTAND...
HUH ?

...HOW YOU FEEL!
WHISH

RANMA! I HAVE A SPECIAL RECIPE IN MIND FOR YOU!
PREPARE YOURSELF!
VMMM
KREEE!

"MEET YOU AT THE FIELD BEHIND THE GYM AFTER SCHOOL..."
IT'S A CHALLENGE!
SOME GUYS JUST DON'T MAKE ANY SENSE...

Part 2

SAUCY REPLY

I HEARD RANMA'S GOING TO FIGHT THE NEW KID!
WE GOTTA SEE THIS!
YAMMER
YAMMER-YAMMER
YAM-YAMMER
RANMA, PREPARE YOURSELF...
WHAT THE HECK?!
CHECK OUT THE RING!
WHAT... WHAT IS IT?!
TUP
HIYA, UCCHAN.

WE ARE HERE...TO DUEL!
SQUENCH
SO **STOP** CALLING ME THAT NAME!
VVM
WHY NOT? I THOUGHT YOU **LIKED** IT WHEN I CALLED YOU THAT!

BUT THE ONE WHO STOLE YOUR CART AND LEFT YOU IN THE DUST WAS MY POP, RIGHT?

SO WHY'RE YOU SO MAD AT M--

SHUT UP!

MR. SAOTOME...

IS THERE SOMETHING YOU'RE NOT TELLING US?

THERE IS.

DUM DUM

WA!
TAKE THIS!
VSH
VSH

YOW!
WRRRRR
TK TK TK TK
FAK

EEEEOW!
HUH?

COOK MINE OVER EASY!
WHOA!

KRAK

OOOOH!!
ALL AROUND THE RING... IT'S A GIANT HOT PLATE!
THIS IS INSANE!
NOW, FOR OKONOMIYAKI UKYO'S SPECIAL RECIPE...
I HOPE YOU LIKE IT!
FLA! A!
SHLORP...
YAA!!
PLAP PLAP
SSSS...

YAA YAA
BLORBLE
WHA-- ?!
MY SPECIAL BATTER... DEEP-DISH GLUE!
AND THIS...
IS RUBBER YAKISOBA NOODLES!
FWONG
FWONG
HYAH!

HISSS
YEE OUCH!

OH, MAN... THAT YAKISOBA SMELLS GOOD!
GO! GO!
MY MOM MAKES OKONOMIYAKI WITH THOSE NOODLES IN IT, TOO!
THAT RANMA'S MAKING ME HUNGRY!

H-HEY, COME ON, NOW!
YIP
WHRR

...MIXED WITH GUNPOWDER !!
POOF
PA PA PA
PA PA PA PA PA PA PA PA PA PA PA PA
RANMA!
IS THIS IT...?
OH, MAN...
I'LL BE NICE... AND NOT SETTLE THIS...
...IN SUCH A DANGEROUS PLACE.
POP POP POP POP
!
SINCE WE...WERE FRIENDS ONCE...
GNNNN

YEARRRR!!
NNNNNNNN...
FWAP
TWANG
SSSSS
YAAAH!!!
BA!
THEY'RE TAKING IT OUT OF THE RING!

OH, WHAT TRAGEDY!

BELOVED FRIENDS SINCE CHILDHOOD! WHY MUST THEY FIGHT EACH OTHER SO!?

BOOM

GET BACK HERE, UKYO!

YOU SISSY!

TATATATA

DA DA DA

ERG!

C'MON! FIGHT LIKE A MAN!

WHY, YOU--!

BOING

THOK

TAP

HYAA!
VISH
WAH!
I TRY TO BE NICE TO YOU AND WHAT DO YOU DO ?!
VOOP
YOU... YOU...
CLUTCH
YOU GOT TO HAVE YOUR FUN ON THAT GRILL...
NOW IT'S MY TURN!
WAIT!
J-JUST A SECOND!
YOU'RE THE ONE...
"WAIT" ?!

BWAH!
POOF
...FORGET THE FLOUR!
NEVER...
BAKING FLOUR
...WHO STARTED THIS!
ZAP
ZAAB
AK!
AK!
IT'S BY THE P.E. EQUIPMENT ROOM!
KA-BOOM
WH-WHAT'S THAT WHITE SMOKE?!
KOFF
KOFF

GOTCHA !!

GLOMP

OH...!

N?

SLAP
HANDS OFF!!
UH...
'SCUSE ME...
ARE THOSE BREASTS...?
NOW WHAT?!

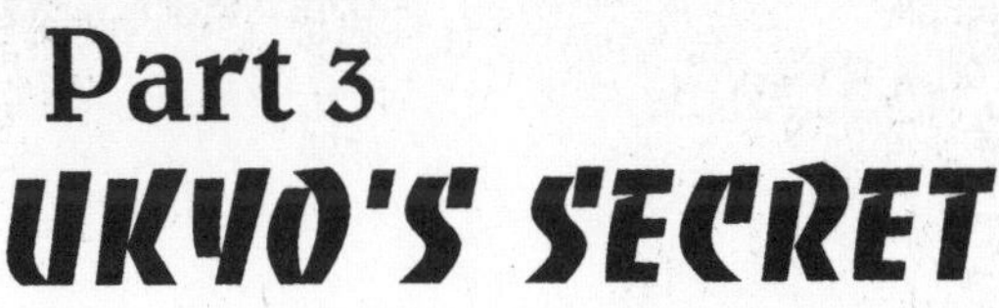

Part 3
UKYO'S SECRET

THAT UKYO GUY... IS A GIRL ?!
NO!
OOOH
GASP
A GIRL ?!

..."CHILDHOOD FRIENDS"...
.....
MAYBE THEY'RE NOT JUST...

TH-THEN THE WAY SHE CAME HUNTING FOR RANMA...
YES, SO HE IS. SHE IS.

P.E. EQUIPMENT ROOM

.....
UKYO... UM...

WHAT KIND OF STUPID QUESTION IS--
"SINCE... WHEN"?
SINCE WHEN... ?
YOU'RE... UH... YOU'RE...
EEEEEEEEE YAA!!
UBBLE UBBLE UBBLE
WHAAP
WHAT'S THE BIG IDEA?!
DOES THE SIGHT OF CLEAVAGE MAKE YOU INSANE ?!
Y-YOU DON'T CHANGE BACK WITH HOT WATER...

BOOM

THIS IS UKYO... YOUR FIANCÉE!

HEH HEH

TOK

ON THAT DAY, MY LIFE AS A WOMAN CAME TO AN END.

OOOOOO

HEARD THE LATEST? UKYO GOT DUMPED BY HER FIANCÉ.
NOT ONLY THAT, HE STOLE THE FAMILY BUSINESS, TOO.
PSST PSST PSST
TSK TSK
NOW SHE'LL NEVER FIND A HUSBAND.
AFTER THAT, ONLY ONE THING MATTERED TO ME...
DEVOTING MY LIFE TO REVENGE!
BOOOM
OKONOMIYAKI BECAME MY LIFE-- I SET UP A PORTABLE GRIDDLE AND COOKED IT BY THE RAGING SEA!
UM...
WHY DID IT HAVE TO BE THE SEA?
ISN'T THAT KINDA POINTLESS?
DOOOM
THAT IS THE POINT, STUPID! DON'T YOU EVER WATCH SAMURAI MOVIES!?
SIZZLE SIZZLE
BA

.....
NO WONDER SHE HATES THEM SO MUCH...
POOR GIRL...

SHE HAS EVERY RIGHT TO HATE.
SIGH
INDEED...

GO AHEAD, UKYO! TAKE OUT ALL YOUR ANGER ON RANMA!
FUNCH

AND HOW D'YOU FIGGER THAT!?
MOOSH
AFTER ALL, IT'S YOUR FAULT TOO!

DESPITE MY AGREEMENT WITH UKYO'S FATHER...
RANMA WAS ALREADY PROMISED TO MARRY AKANE.
P.E. ROOM
YET I DID NOT WANT TO GIVE UP THE OKONOMIYAKI CART.
BEING UNABLE TO MAKE THAT DECISION FOR HIM...
I HAD TO TRUST THE BOY TO CHOOSE ON HIS OWN.
WHA-?
HUH?
!
RANMA, YOU CHOSE AKANE EVEN BACK THEN...?
.....
I DON'T REMEMBER ANY OF THIS!

RANMA, M'BOY... LISTEN WELL AND ANSWER YOUR FATHER.
WHICH DO YOU LIKE BETTER? UKYO OR OKONOMIYAKI?
HMMM...
OKONOMIYAKI!
AND THAT ANSWER MADE THE DECISION FOR--
BONK
YES, SHE HAS EVERY RIGHT...
WAIT! WAIT! I DON'T EVEN *REMEMBER* ALL THAT!
WELL, REMEMBER *THIS*!!

GRRR
GRRR
ENEMIES TO ALL WOMEN!
"ENEMIES TO"..WAIT A MINUTE!
TALK ABOUT DYSFUNCTIONAL FAMILIES!
YOU TWO ARE DISGUSTING!

WELL, I GUESS THEY'VE GOT IT COMING.
WHAP
POOM
WE DON'T CARE!!
SCREE SCREE
I DIDN'T EVEN KNOW UKYO WAS A GIRL TILL...
BA-BONK

HUH?
UKYO'S GONE TOO.
HE'S ESCAPED!
RANMA'S GONE!
!
HEY!

VROOOOMM
WHERE DO YOU THINK YOU'RE GOING ?!
JUST FOLLOW ME.

THERE IT IS.

FONG

HERE. YOUR SPATULA.
TAK.

I WON'T MAKE ANY EXCUSES.
DO WHAT YOU WANT TO ME.

HEH. ALL RIGHT THEN...
RRRR

EXPECT NO MERCY!
WHEN YOU ABANDONED ME...
KRAK
YOU MADE IT IMPOSSIBLE FOR ME TO EVER AGAIN EMBRACE MY OWN FEMININITY!
UH...
VMMMM
WHOA! DON'T YOU THINK YOU'RE OVERREACTING?
VSH
VSH
SHUT UP!!
WATCH YOURSELF, RANMA...
TAP
SINCE THAT DARK DAY...
VIP

SHAH

...I'VE SWORN THAT I WILL NEVER...

WHISH

DUCK

...LOVE ANOTHER MAN!!

WHAT A WASTE.

A CUTE GIRL LIKE YOU.

POKE

ERRK

WHO'DVE THOUGHT LITTLE "UCCHAN" WOULD GROW UP SO CUTE ?

BLUSH

CUTE...

TOO BAD NO GUY WILL EVER--

BOOM

YOU'RE LYING! I'M **NOT** CUTE!!

BLUSH

IT'S NOT A LIE. YOU ARE CU--

VOOM

WHACK

STOP IT!!

BLUSH

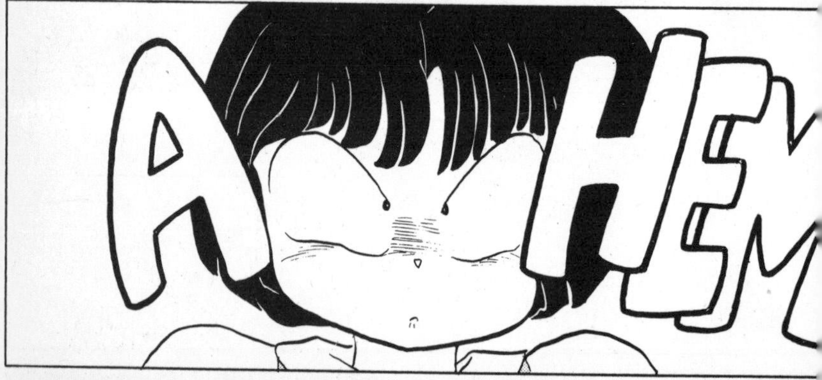

WH-WHAT'S WITH YOU, AKANE?

YOU MUST BE HAPPY... NOW THAT YOU HAVE A CUTE FIANCÉE!

SO. YOU'RE AKANE.

YEP. CUTE FIANCÉE, MEET UNCUTE FIANCÉE.
PAT
S-S-SO WHAT...?

JAB
SO WHAT IF I'M NOT CUTE?!
TOMBOY!
JAB
.....

SO YOU TWO AREN'T GETTING ALONG?

GEE, IS IT THAT OBVIOUS!?
AM I RIGHT? UNCUTE OR WHAT?

PAP
WHSHH

LET'S BE FRIENDS AGAIN... STARTING TOMORROW!
LET'S LET BYGONES BE BYGONES, SHALL WE?
VVIP

UH... RIGHT...
YOU MUST BE VERY HAPPY.

Part 4

RYOGA VS. UKYO

'MORNING!
HEY, HEAR ABOUT RANMA?
BLAH BLAH
WHAT, YOU MEAN HIS NEW FIANCÉE?
EVERYONE'S TALKING ABOUT IT.
AIN'T YOU GOT ALL THE LUCK.
WHADDYA NEED TWO FOR!?
WHAT'RE YOU TALKING ABOUT?!
I HAD ENOUGH PROBLEMS WITH JUST AN UNCUTE FIANCÉE!
OH, SO?
THEN WHY DON'T YOU SWITCH TO THE CUTE ONE?!
VIP VIP
BOING BOING

SPLAAAAT

OFFICIAL SOUVENIR KOUNTRY KILNS™ of JAPAN

MOOSH

I HEARD THE RUMORS.

HWOOOOO
AKANE...
UH... RYOGA... ?
GASP
OOOH!

YOU MEAN ABOUT THE OTHER FIANCÉE...?
RUMORS ?

I WILL NOT HAVE IT!!
PSST! NO WAY!
WHAT SHE SAID.
IT'S OKAY. I DON'T CARE WHO RANMA GOES OUT WITH.
CREEEK...
OH! GAK!

EVEN IF THE OTHER FIANCÉE...

I WILL NOT SEE AKANE INSULTED BY A TWO-TIMING LOUT!

NOW YOU'VE DONE IT! NOBODY GETS AWAY WITH SAYIN' THAT I...

SHAH

SHAH

WHSH
WHSH
TAK
TAK
TAK.
YOW!
I WON'T STAND BY AND HAVE MY ENGAGEMENT RIDICULED!
HUH?
THAT VOICE...
TAKE IT BACK!
VOOSH
GYAA!
UKYO!
GASP

STOP!

WOULD YOU HIT A **GIRL**!?

WHA...?

A GIRL... !?
FEH.
SWAP
AS IF I DON'T KNOW A MAN WHEN I SEE ONE!
TWOK
TANG
TWOK
TANG
WHAT ?!
HIYAAAA!
VWOO
GOTCHA!
WHO'RE YOU CALLING A MAN?! FLOUR BOMB!
BOOF
GWAH!

ZUNG
TAKE THIS!
SHH
AK...!
OOOOH!
FWP...

RYOGA, DON'T--!
IT'S OVER!
AHHH!
GULP!
CHECK 'EM OUT. STILL THINK "HE" IS A GUY!?
BAZOOM
EEP...
GET LOST!
BOOM
OH, RYOGA...
SHOWING MY CHEST TO ANOTHER MAN! YOUR OWN FIANCÉE!
HEY. DIDN'T I JUST SAVE YOU?
HEH.
BACH
OOOH!

SCHOOL NURSE

NN... ?

OH, THANK GOODNESS... HOW ARE YOU FEELING, RYOGA?

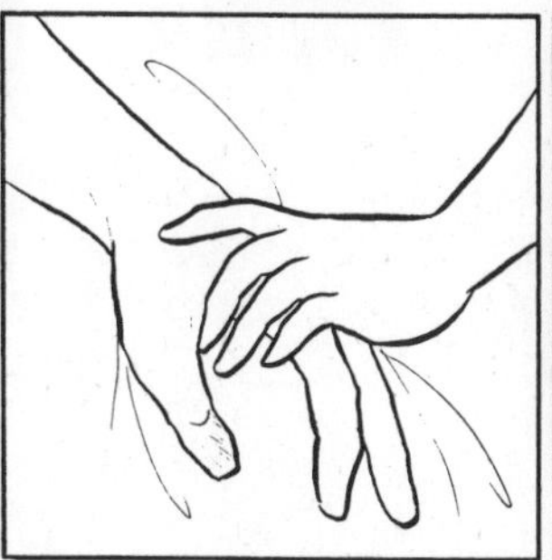

.....
BADUMP
BADUMP
BADUMP
.....
SOBB
AKANE
!!

HEH
HEH
HEH.
POP
BIFF
BAFF
BOOM
AK!
UGH!!
OOF!!
HM
?

WOOM
RANMA HONEY...
WHAT WERE YOU THINKING !?
HMPH !
huf huf huf
SHOOP
HONESTLY !

"DON'T WORRY ABOUT US..."

SIGH.
AKANE.

"DON'T WORRY ABOUT US," SHE SAYS!? AAAAARGH!
BOOM BOOM BOOM
HEY HEY HEY!

SHE DOESN'T KNOW HOW I FEEL!
WHACH

WHAT'S GOT YOU SO WORKED UP?
POST

YOU'RE IN LOVE WITH AKANE, AREN'T YOU.
WH...
ERK!

WHY... YOU... !
JAB
HOLD IT! I'M ON YOUR SIDE!

LET ME INTRODUCE MYSELF PROPERLY.
I'M UKYO... RANMA HONEY'S CUTE FIANCÉE.

OKONOMIYAKI UCCHAN'S
CHAN'S

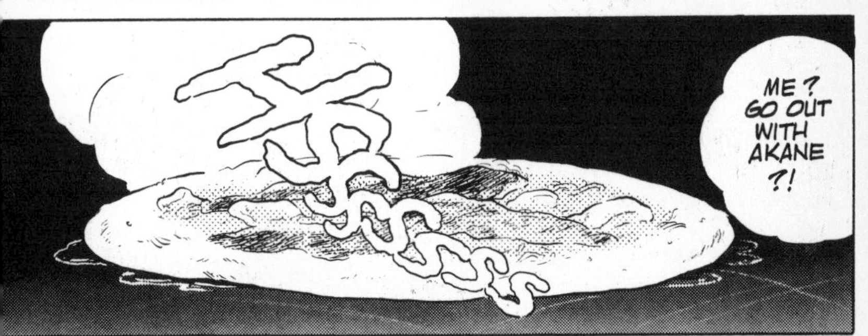
ME? GO OUT WITH AKANE ?!

I'LL SET IT UP FOR YOU!
FWIP
WHY? SHE'LL ONLY SAY NO ANYWAY.

COWARD.
BAM
WHA DID YOU SAY !?

THAT'S A HOT GRILL.

JUST LEAVE IT TO ME.
I PROMISE I'LL GET AKANE TO GO OUT WITH YOU.
SO, "PROMISE," EH...?

I WONDER IF RYOGA LEFT ON ANOTHER TRIP...
SOMETHIN' TELLS ME...
...HE'S A LOT CLOSER THAN YOU THINK.
KWEE
KWEE KWEE

Part 5

LOVE LETTERS IN THE SAUCE

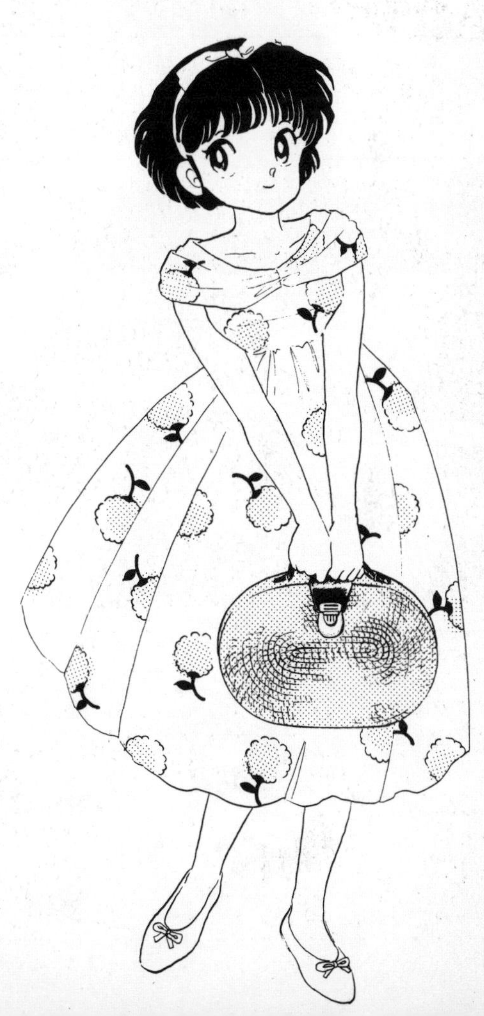

AKANE AND RYOGA ARE GOING TO HAVE A WONDERFUL DATE...

OKONOMIYAKI
Uc cha n's

IF I HAVE ANYTHING TO SAY ABOUT IT!

SSS SSS

AFTER ALL, IF THEY HIT IT OFF...

...RANMA WILL BELONG TO *ME!*

SPLP

HEH. A LOVE LETTER NO ONE COULD RESIST!

Akane: meet me at Ucchan's Okonomiyaki at 2 pm today --Ryoga

SSSSSSS

TENDO
TRAINING
HALL
天道道場
AKANE! ♪
HM ?
THAT VOICE...
Ucchan's
A FRIEND OF YOURS, AKANE ?
OH, DAD! LET ME INTRODUCE YOU!
SKRATCH SKRATCH
THIS IS RANMA'S *CUTE* FIANCÉE... UKYO KUONJI.
THE CUTE ONE, IS IT...?
SHIK SHIK...
GOOD MORNING AND NICE TO MEET YOU.

--ANGRY !!

DOOOOM

PWORK

P-TOO!

CAR

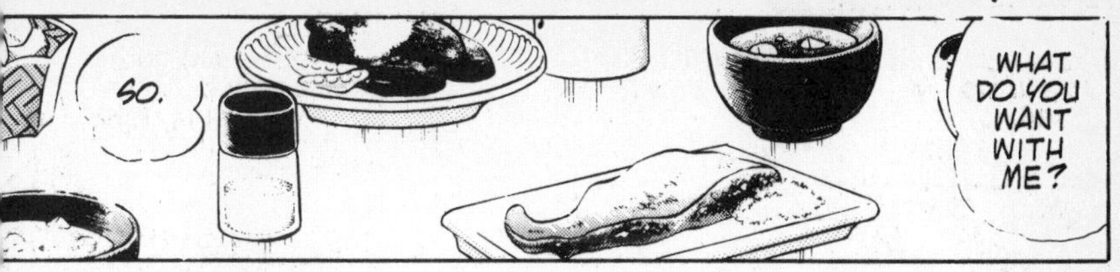
WHAT DO YOU WANT WITH ME?
SO.

NOW LISTEN...
YOU KNOW, RANMA HONEY! YOU DON'T MIND NOT BEING HIS FIANCÉE ANYMORE, DO YOU?
KLAK

"RAN-CHAN"?
BE HONEST, AKANE. THINGS AREN'T GOING WELL WITH YOU AND RAN-CHAN, ARE THEY?

.....
DON'T TELL ME YOU REALLY LOVE EACH OTHER!

--WITH A MACHO CHICK LIKE HER? GET REAL!
VIP
VIP
HOLD IT, YOU!
VROOOM
NO! HE COULDN'T POSSIBLY BE IN LOVE WITH--
BAM

PONG
HOW'D YOU GUESS?
THEN YOU'RE NOT IN LOVE?

TARAN TA RAAAA
BOP
THIS IS *YOUR* MESS, IDIOT! FIX IT!
YOU DO REALIZE WHAT WILL HAPPEN...

A NOTE-- ?!

CHOMP

WOP

"MEET ME AT UCCHAN'S AT 2:00 P.M. TODAY."
Okonomiyaki at 2 pm today.
"AKANE...

WAIT A MINUTE... YOU'RE SETTING UP AKANE AND RYOGA FOR A DATE ?!
I JUST GAVE HER THE LOVE-NOTE.
YUP.

A CHALLENGE !
SNARF SNARF SNARF

NO WAY AKANE'S GONNA SHOW!
YOU SOUND AWFULLY SURE OF YOURSELF.

HEH. I GUESS YOU HAVEN'T HEARD...

...THAT AKANE'S THE BIGGEST MACHO DWEEB IN THE HISTORY OF JAPAN!

OH, HE ASKED ME OUT! HE REALLY ASKED ME OUT!
TEE HEE!
GIGGLE
OH, I HOPE I HAVE SOMETHING PRETTY ENOUGH TO WEAR!

IF YOU CAN GET AKANE ACTING LIKE THAT...
heh

...I'LL DRESS UP LIKE A GIRL AND RUN AROUND THE NEIGHBORHOOD A HUNDRED TIMES!
WAHAHAHA
GASP!!

...COULD POSSIBLY EXIST...!
I NEVER DREAMED SUCH AN UNFEMININE GIRL...

...IF HE WERE HALF AS MANLY AS AKANE!
HE'D BE TWICE THE MAN HE IS...
BOING BOING

CAN'T EVEN ASK HER OUT ON HIS OWN!
AND RYOGA...

OH NO...
THAT CHANGES EVERYTHING...
STAGGER

...CAN'T EVEN FIND TOKYO.
Please don't talk to the Horses
ZEEE ZEEE
WHERE IS UCCHAN'S OKONOMIYAKI SHOP?!
MEANWHILE, RYOGA...

CHAKAASSSHH

YOU DON'T MIND NOT BEING HIS FIANCÉE ANYMORE, DO YOU?
YEAH, RIGHT.
SHE SHOWS UP FROM OUT OF NOWHER AND--
HIYAAA!
DOOOM

I'LL BE THERE, UKYO!
WHAK

BUMM

RANMA...
ISN'T IT ALMOST TIME? DON'T YOU HAVE TO GET READY?

I DON'T SEE THAT IT'S ANY BUSINESS OF YOURS, RANMA.

IN FACT, TAKE MY ADVICE... AND STAY OUT OF OUR WAY!
OH, RIGHT, LIKE I'D...

"OUR WAY"?!

NO.
Y-YOU'RE NOT REALLY GOING...?

WHAT ELSE CAN I DO... AFTER A NOTE LIKE THAT?!
GAA!

HEY, S-SINCE WHEN DID YOU TURN INTO A...
THIS IS WHAT I LIVE FOR!
JAB JAB

AND ONE MORE THING, RANMA...

I DON'T CARE WHO IS...OR ISN'T... YOUR FIANCÉE.
.....
THAT'S NOT WHY I'M DOING...
HUH ?
FOOEY. SO SHE DOESN'T CARE, EH?
BWAHAHAHA! HOW DO YOU LIKE THAT, RANMA!?
JUST STAY OUT OF OUR WAY, OKAY? TEE-HEE!
NO WAY. NO... WAY...
...YOU GET AWAY WITH THIS!
BLOOSH

SLAM
Ucchan's
I'M HERE!
AKANE!
OH, I'M SO HAPPY YOU CAME!
OF COURSE I CAME!
YAKI
HUH?
THEN THAT MEANS YOU HAVE SOME FEELINGS FOR HIM AFTER ALL!
Heh
WHAT ARE YOU TALKING AB--
ZHOOOOOP

I...

I MADE IT...

RUH...

RYOGA...?

FWOMP

AND HOW MANY WEEKS AGO WAS THAT?
UH... THANKS... ?
I BOUGHT THEM AS I LEFT THE HOUSE.
AHEM
WILT

IN HONOR OF YOUR FIRST DATE...
Love
SSSSSSSS

SHE'S TRYING TO SET ME UP WITH HIM...
NOW I GET IT!
SHUDDER
TREMBLE
OUR FIRST... WHAT ?
..THIS ONE'S ON ME.

DOES SHE REALLY THINK I'LL FALL FOR THAT?
...SO SHE CAN HAVE RANMA TO HERSELF!

AND HERE'S POOR, GOOD-HEARTED RYOGA, CAUGHT IN HER SCHEME...

PEEK
......

......
AHEM
FIDGET FIDGET

IT'S... IT'S GOOD... ISN'T IT? HEE HEE HEE HEE HEE HEE HEE!
SNARF SNARF SNARF
WAHA HAHA HAHA HA!

SO THEY THINK THEY'RE GONNA HAVE A DATE, EH?! NOT WHEN I GET THROUGH WITH 'EM!
Salon 3F
NYAHA HAHA HAHA HA!
SHOOM

Part 6

RYOGA'S WHAT?!

OKONOMIYAKI
Uc chan's
PARTY
OKAY!
PRIVATE PARTY
YOU KIDS BE GOOD WHILE I'M GONE!
HIROSHIMA-STYLE SPECIAL ¥500
HUH?
HEY!
BOING

OHHHH... I SEE IT NOW...

UKYO TALKED HIM INTO THIS...HE REALLY DOESN'T WANT TO BE HERE...

IF YOU LIKE HER, STUPID, JUST TELL HER!

PSS PSS PSS PSS

HOW CAN I DO THAT IF I DON'T KNOW IF SHE LIKES ME BACK?!

IN WHAT? IN WHAT?!
IN FACT, I'VE ALWAYS BEEN IN... IN...
I DO WANT TO!
HE DOES WANT TO!
HUF HUF
HUF
TONK
WHA...?
BOOM
YOU TWO-TIMER!!
TOOM TOOM
HOW DARE YOU GO OUT WITH HER...

FIANCÉE!

I...AM RYOGA'S...

GASP

HWOOOO
FIANCÉE ?!
BOOOM
KLANG
KLANG
KLANG
H-HOW COULD I NOT KNOW...
...THAT I HAD A FIANCÉE ?!
IT'S NOT YOUR FAULT YOU DON'T KNOW.
YOU SEE...

.....
WONK
...WE WERE BUT BABES WHEN OUR PARENTS ARRANGED OUR UNION!

DON'T JUST SIT THERE!
WHAT AM I GOING TO DOOOO...?
KLANG KLANG KLANG
WONK
JUST WHAT DO YOU THINK YOU'RE DOING?
GRRRR!
WHY DID YOU DO THAT, YOU VIOLENT GIRL YOU!

BOOM
I'M IN LOVE WITH AKANE!

NO...I WILL HESITATE NO LONGER!

ARE YOU GOING TO LET SOME GIRL COME OUT OF NOWHERE AND CLAIM YOUR FIANCÉE?!
OH!

WHA...
?
AKANE
!!
VIP
I AM
IN L--
WH-WHAT
ARE YOU
DOING?!
?
BA-BUMP
BA-BUMP
SPLOOSH
IF YOU
TRY TO
LEAVE
ME...

GYAAH! CUT IT OUT!
...I'LL DO THIS!!
SHOOM SHOOM
KLATTER
SPLISH
SPLASH
UM...
SHK SHK
THAT LITTLE... AND JUST WHEN AKANE AND RYOGA WERE ABOUT TO GET TOGETHER, TOO! WELL...
H-HEY, LEGGO!
OH, RYOGA, WE MUST ESCAPE THOSE WHO ENVY OUR LOVE!
WHOA!
SHA
...JUST LET HER TRY!
GLOMP
VRRRMMMM
SHA
TONNG

YOU... YOU...

YOU WON'T GET AWAY !!

.....

KEEP OFF GRASS

I'M YOUR FIANCÉE!
MAN, THIS IS FUN!

WHAT A MAROON! HE STILL HASN'T FIGURED THIS OUT!
H-H-HOW DO YOU KN-KN-KNOW ABOUT...?

BLUSH
SHOULDN'T I KNOW EVERYTHING ABOUT THE MAN I'LL MARRY?

WOBBLE
SHE... SHE KNOWS! AND YET...

SIGH
...YOU STILL WANT ME?!
WHA-- ?!

YOU'VE MADE ME...SO HAPPY!
PAK
WHOA! WHOA! DON'T GET WEIRD ON ME!

WHY YOU'RE...
WHO DO YOU THINK I AM?!

AAAARGH!
...THE GIRL I'M GOING TO MARRY!
GOOSH

HM ?
FLAPPA
GET OFFA ME, YOU PERVERT !!
BIFF BAM POW

ZEE ZEE
JEEZ... THAT WAS CLOSE!

OH...!

POOOM
RYOGA
!

POOR RYOGA...
YOU DON'T DESERVE TO BE MIXED UP IN THIS.

GWAAAA!

KLOK
IS THERE SOME REASON YOU HATE RYOGA?

SORRY YOUR DATE DIDN'T WORK OUT. HEH.
WH... ?
KEEP OFF GRASS

IT... CAN'T BE.

RANMA... WERE YOU JEALOUS ?!

WHAT?! I KNEW YOU WERE EASY, BUT WHEN DID YOU GO INSANE?!
"EASY"... ?

RUSHING OFF TO SEE RYOGA JUST 'CAUSE HE DRIBBLED YOU A LOVE LET-TER IN SAUCE?

AND WHO ARE YOU TO TALK...
BLORBLE

IF THAT'S THE WAY YOU SEE ME...
WELL, FINE!

A DATE...
I THOUGHT IT WAS A DUEL!

OUCH!
...YOU PERVERT ?!
BOOT

ICE CREAM
GIGGLE GIGGLE
TEE HEE
.....
SHFF SHFF
PLEASE PUT TRASH WHERE IT

...THEY'D THINK I WAS SOME KINDA PERVERT!
IF ANYBODY SAW ME, DRESSED AS AS A GIRL...
GASP!
BOOF

SHE COULDN'T JUST BOOT ME, SHE HAD TO SPLASH ME FIRST.
STUPID... MACHO... DWEEB!
SHFF

PERVERT! GET HIM!!
EH?
NO! WAIT! STOP!
WHAK BOOM POW BAM
PEEK
RAN-CHAN!

WHAT WERE YOU DOING THERE?
JJJJJ
STUPID... AKANE...!

STUPID RANMA!
JUST FOR THAT, I WILL DATE RYOGA!
JJJJJJ

Part 7

AT LONG LAST...THE DATE!

OH MY!
AKANE'S REALLY ON A DATE WITH RYOGA?
THEY SEEM TO BE HITTING IT OFF TOO.
TENDO TRAINING HALL
無差別格闘流
天道道場

SHE'LL BE FINE. SHE'S STRONG AS A BULL.
FEH
SERIOUSLY, RANMA... WHY DON'T YOU GO AND GET AKANE?
RAAAAAN-MAAAAA!
OOOO WOOOO
RANMA... I **REALLY** THINK YOU SHOULD GO.
UH... YEAH...

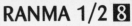

GET REAL!
THEN YOU'LL RESCUE HER IF SHE'S IN TROUBLE, RAN-CHAN?
REALTY
Beauty Salon
UGS
CAFE Rendezvous
I'M SORRY, RYOGA.
WUH...?
I HOPE IT'S NOT TOO MUCH TROUBLE FOR YOU!
MAKING YOU COME WITH ME LIKE THIS...

TH-THIS HAS TO BE...
A DREAM!

AKANE ASKING ME OUT LIKE THIS...

...IT CAN'T REALLY BE HAPPENING!

I'LL AWAKEN AND IT WILL ALL BE GONE!
HEY! NO HEADBANGING ALLOWED!
BONG BONG BONG
SPOOT

KRIKKLE
TAKTAK

IT DIDN'T HURT... IT IS A DREAM.
SOB
RRRMMM

RUMBLE RUMBLE
KONG
RUN!

BLBLLLLL
POINK
R...RYOGA...?

THAT HURT...
...A LITTLE...

WHY DON'T WE...GO SOMEWHERE ELSE?
IT'S NOT A DREAM!

THEY SEEM TO BE HAVING FUN.
RRUMBLE
POP
HMPH

TWEET TWEET

BOAT RENTALS
HEY!
COME ON, LET'S RENT A BOAT!
ERK
BE AWFUL IF YOU FELL IN, WOULDN'T IT... P-CHAN?
POIK!
BOOM

QUIT FOLLOWING US AROUND!
.....
RANMA AND I ARE ON OUR OWN DATE.
OH?
NO FISHING
DON'T YOU MIND US NOW!
16
SO FIRST HE TRIES TO KEEP RYOGA AND ME APART...
...THEN HE TURNS AROUND AND ASKS YOU OUT, EH?!
WHOOM
WHOA.
NO FISHING
11
SPLAT

RAN-CHAN!
BLOOSH
YOU TWO-TIMER. YOU'VE LOST ALL RIGHT TO CALL YOURSELF AKANE'S FIANCÉ!
BLBLBLBL...
OOSH
EEK!
WHO IS A TWO-TIMER... RYOGA?!

SPLASH
HOW DARE YOU DO THIS WHEN YOU HAVE *ME*?!
.....
WHA ?
WHA ?
WHA ?
HUH HUH HUH

WHEN YOU JUMPED ALL OVER ME...

...WAS THAT JUST A *LARK*?!
WAP WAP WAP
I WAS... I WAS...
SKRITCH SKRITCH

SHE *KNOWS*... BUT STILL *LOVES* ME!
HOW CAN I EVER HOPE TO FIND ANOTHER GIRL WHO'LL... WHO'LL...
WELL, I STILL WANT YOU... EVEN IF YOU'RE A *PIG*!
SOBB

HOW MANY TIMES DO YOU HAVE TO GET IN THE WAY, GIRL?!
WOOSH
YOW!
DUCK

YOU'RE THE ONLY ONE FOR ME!
SKWISH
ARE YOU SURE YOU'RE SURE?!

I THINK YOU SHOULD RUN, RANMA.
WHAT? WHO'S RANMA?

IT'S... YOU...!
HM?

C'MON, RYOGA! CANTCHA TAKE A JOKE?
RANMA...?
KRAK KRAK
RAAAAN-MAAAA!

WHOA!
JAB
YOU WILL DIE!!

COMP
I WILL NOT...
PLOOSH

...GET WET!
KONK

BLURRRBLE
BOING
BOING
EEEEEEK!
100% Fruit
FRUIT TIME

TAP
HWOOOOOO
.....

NO MATTER THE CAUSE...FOR A BRIEF MOMENT, MY HEART BETRAYED AKANE...

RANMA, YOU'RE SUCH A JERK!

KWEEEE

DO YOU HAVE *FUN* TORMENTING RYOGA?

SPLAT

I'M SO SORRY, RYOGA.

RANMA'S SUCH A...

AKANE..

GOODBYE.

I CAN SEE YOU... NO MORE.

HHSSSHHHH H H

Sprinkler in Use*

RANMA, YOU BE SURE TO APOLOGIZE WHEN RYOGA COMES BACK.

I THINK HE'S ALREADY GOTTEN OVER IT.

THIS IS FUN NO MATTER ***HOW*** MANY TIMES I DO IT!

BLUB BLUB BLUB

BITE BITE BITE BITE BITE BITE

Part 8

HAPPOSAI DAYS ARE HERE AGAIN

HHHSSSS

EEEEEK! BIKINI THIEF!

MM ?

SHHHH
GIVE IT BACK!
YOU PERVERT!
EEEEEE
EEEE
EEEEE
VRROOMM
SNAK SHACK
YOU SENILE DELINQUENT!
WHOMP
FOOEY. WELL, IF I CAN'T GO TREASURE HUNTING, I'M GOING GIRL-HUNTING!
HHSSSSH

EEEEEEE
PRETTY LADIES!
EEEEEEEEE
WANTA EAT SOME WATERMELON?!
EEEEEEE
FWO
WHERE DO YOU GET YOUR ENERGY?
WHERE DO YOU THINK?
BLUE SKIES!
WHITE CLOUDS!
BRIGHT SUN!
I LOVE THE SEA!
SIGH
IF YOU'RE LOOKING FOR THE CLOUDS, THEY'RE BEHIND YOU.
AAAH! I FEEL SO YOUNG!
GROPE GROPE
GROPE GROPE
GWAAAAAAH!

BOOOT
THERE MUST BE SOME WAY TO CALM HIM DOWN...
HUF HUF
CAT CAFE
AIYAAA!
NIHAO, RANMA!
VACANCY
CAT CAFE
SHAMPOO...
CHILLED RAMEN!? OVER HERE!
BOT
BOT

I SO HAPPY! RANMA COME TO BEACH AFTER SHAMPOO!
PRR PRR PRR
GOOSH
IT'S A COINCIDENCE!
WHAT ARE YOU TWO GIRLS DOING?!

OH, SO YOU DO BUSINESS ON THE BEACH DURING SUMMER...
RANMA, YOU DATE WITH SHAMPOO AFTER WORK?

DATE HUH?
I GOT IT!

SAY WHAT?!
YOU'LL INTRODUCE ME TO A G-GIRL?!
INN

IT'S TOO GOOD TO BE TRUE!
IT'S TRUE! SO LAY OFF THE BIKINI STEALING FOR A WHILE!
point

DUMP
LUCKY I BROUGHT MY TREASURE CHEST ALONG!
NO TOUCH
MY PRECIOUS

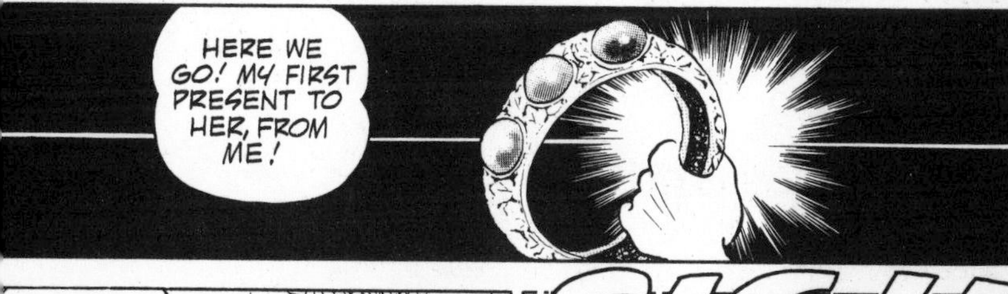
HERE WE GO! MY FIRST PRESENT TO HER, FROM ME!

LISTEN, RANMA, MY TYPE HAS LONG HAIR AND BIG EYES...
YEP, THAT SOUNDS JUST LIKE HER.
SIGH
RANMA! YOU'RE NOT GOING TO INTRODUCE HIM TO SHAMPOO!?

PUBLIC SHOWE
CAT CAFE
CHINESE NOODLES
SODA
FLAP FLAP
YOU THINK SO?
SHE'LL TURN HIM DOWN FLAT!
BLUSH
YO, SHAMPOO.
RANMA!
GETTING A FEW STEPS AHEAD OF YOURSELF, AREN'T YOU?
OH, WHAT A WIFE SHE'LL MAKE...
I'D LIKE TO INTRODUCE A FRIEND OF MINE...
RAMUNE 200
ICE 150
RAMEN 500
POIK!

HE SAY HE WANT DATE WITH YOU, GREAT-GRANDMOTHER.
THERE. DO I DELIVER, OR WHAT?
OH YEAH?
BIG EYES!
LONG HAIR!
BRRR BRRR BRRR
WHO IS THIS OLD FREAK?
BOO HOO HOO HOO HOO
TEARS OF HAPPINESS, OLD MAN?
OF COURSE! SHAMPOO'S GREAT-GRANDMOTHER IS THE PERFECT AGE FOR HIM!
IS GOOD COUPLE.

LET'S LEAVE THESE LOVEBIRDS ALONE.
AND WE KIDS GO PLAY!
STOP!

THIS IS FOR A DOWRY.
BOING
AIYAA, IS BEAUTIFUL BRACELET!

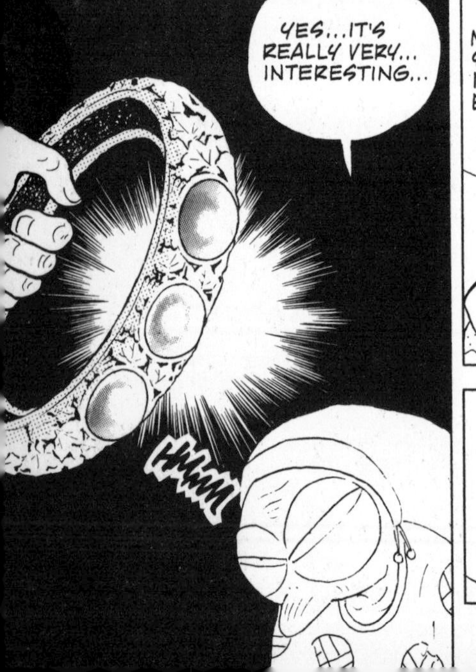
YES...IT'S REALLY VERY... INTERESTING...

NOW THAT YOU MENTION IT, IT LOOKS EXPENSIVE.
DID YOU STEAL IT?
HOW DARE YOU!

THIS IS A MEMENTO OF MY FIRST LOVE.
SIGH
OH...?

...I MET A BEAUTIFUL VILLAGE GIRL WHO STOLE MY HEART!

Happosai, age 18

OH, GIVE ME A BREAK!

PLEASE, TAKE THIS TO REMEMBER ME!
WOOSH

THAT WAS THE LAST I SAW OF HER...
YES, YES...
...A TRAGIC STORY, INDEED...

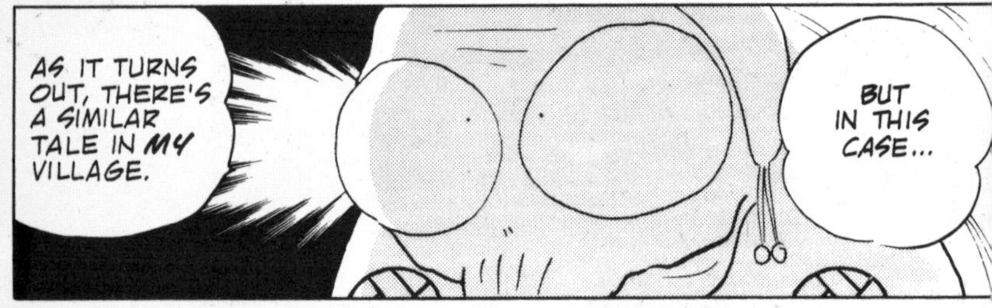
AS IT TURNS OUT, THERE'S A SIMILAR TALE IN *MY* VILLAGE.
BUT IN THIS CASE...

THE MAN HIT ON EVERY GIRL IN THE VILLAGE...
...AND GOT TURNED DOWN BY ALL OF THEM...
EEK
EEK
EEK
...SO HE STOLE ALL OUR VALUABLES AND RAN AWAY!
GET 'IM!
GET 'IM!
TSK TSK.
WHAT A HORRIBLE MAN.

HWOOO

SQUINT

WELL, YOU OUGHT TO KNOW...

...YOU CRIMINAL!

HO!

SSSS SSSSS
OH!
OH!
TOP

LIFE'S JUST FULL OF SURPRISES.
MAYBE INTRODUCING THEM WAS A BAD IDEA.

WHAT?
YOU WILL RETURN THAT FAMILY HEIRLOOM.

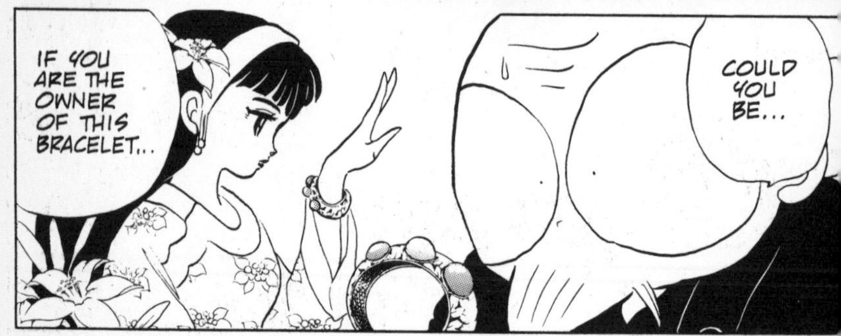
COULD YOU BE...
IF YOU ARE THE OWNER OF THIS BRACELET...

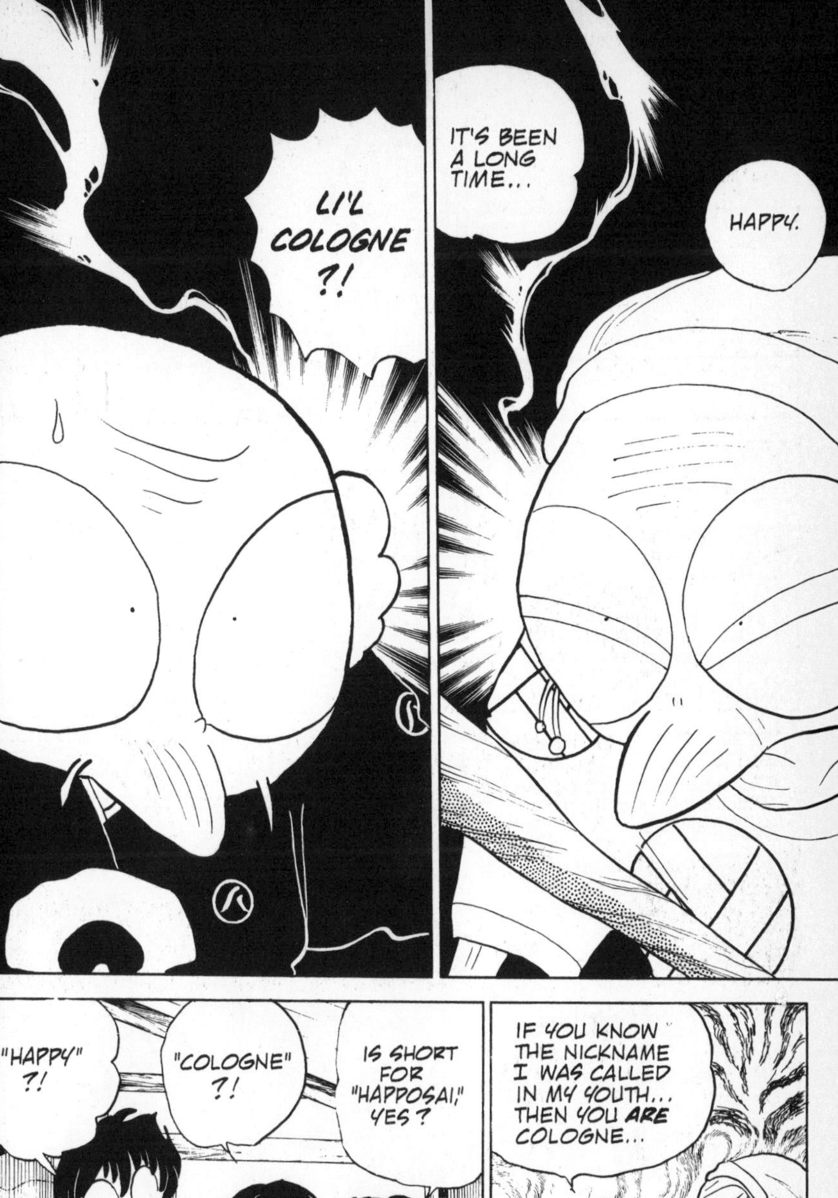

LI'L COLOGNE ?!
IT'S BEEN A LONG TIME...
HAPPY.
"HAPPY" ?!
"COLOGNE" ?!
IS SHORT FOR "HAPPOSAI," YES?
IF YOU KNOW THE NICKNAME I WAS CALLED IN MY YOUTH... THEN YOU **ARE** COLOGNE...

POOF

FAREWELL YOUTH!

WAH! A SMOKE SCREEN!

WA HA HA HA HA

NOW THAT I KNOW IT'S AN HEIRLOOM--I'LL NEVER RETURN IT!

YOU... YOU... MONSTE !

SHAMPOO, YOU MUST GET THAT BRACELET BACK BEFORE HE DISCOVERS ITS SECRET!

SECRET...?

IF YOU FAIL...

...THIS WORLD WILL BECOME A LIVING HELL!

WHAT?!

BRR BRR BRR

Part 9
ONE MOMENT
TO LOVE

SO THE SECRET OF THE BRACELET...
HISSSHHH!
...IS ITS LOVE PILLS?
CORRECT.
SHKK
SHKK
SHKK

THERE ARE PILLS IMBEDDED IN THAT BRACELET...
...WHICH, IF SWALLOWED...
...MAKE THE SWALLOWER FALL IN LOVE WITH THE FIRST PERSON OF THE OPPOSITE SEX HE OR SHE SEES!
WHOO...
HOW TERRIFYING...
SHKK
SHKK
SHKK
IF HAPPY DISCOVERS THOSE PILLS...
...THEN IT REALLY WILL BE HELL ON EARTH!
NYEH HEHE HEH!
FLAP FLAP

SPOING
NYEHEHEH!
I HEARD YOU, I HEARD YOU!
CURSE YOU, HAPPY!
SOUV
SHAVED ICE

OH, SHAMPOO, BABY!
NIHAO!

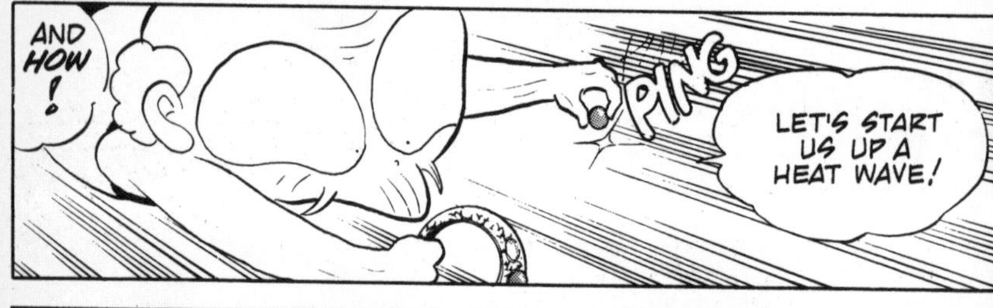
AND HOW!
PING
LET'S START US UP A HEAT WAVE!

AAAAAAH...

SPLAT
VIP

I GOT YOU NOW, FREAK!

NO!! IT'S A TRAP!!
BADGEGILL

HOI!
WHOP
WAHAHAHA
HE GOT AWAY!

HOW DARE YOU TREAT YOUR MASTER SO!
KLONG

SO THAT'S THE FAMOUS LOVE PILL, EH...?
BUT HE DROP ONE.

LET SEE IF PILL REALLY WORK.
POP

......
WHOMPF

NO GET IN WAY!
OH? DID I GET IN YOUR WAY?

HM?

MAN... YOU'RE CUTE!
HUH?

...MAKE THE SWALLOWER FALL IN LOVE WITH THE FIRST PERSON OF THE OPPOSITE SEX HE OR SHE SEES!

N-NO... WAIT...
BLUSH!
I MEAN WAY CUTE!

ONLY KIDDING!
MYAAAAH!

TH-THAT'S THE LOVE PILL TALKING, IT'S NOT REALLY--
NOT LIKE THIS!
FLUTTER FLUTTER

WHSH WHSH
BWAHAHAHAHAHA!
YOU FELL FOR IT, YOU DUMMY!

WHAP
GLMP!
How's it going, son?

YOU THINK I'D ACTUALLY SWALLOW THIS THING ?!

LOOK... WHAT YOU MADE ME DO...!
WOBBLE
SHOWERS
LOC
SOB
VROOM
RANMA, YOU LOOK SHAMPOO!
OH NO, YOU DON'T!
YOU OLD GHOUL!
JERK
YOU'VE GOT TO HAVE AN ANTI... ANTI...
GASP

HOW... HOW COULD I...
HOW COULD I NEVER SEE...
point
...JUST HOW LOVELY A WOMAN IN FULL BLOOM CAN BE!?
GREAT-GRANDMOTHER, NO FAIR!
GLOMP
OH, YOU DON'T MEAN IT!
GASP! OH MY GAWD

YOU STAY AWAY!
HYAH
NEVER!
NO ONE WILL EVER COME BETWEEN US!
ZIP
NOW, COLOGNE!
VOOM
YOU MUST MARRY ME! NOW!
RANMA!
RANMA SERIOUS!
N-NO!
NOOOO!
RANMA, DON'T GO!

HOLD IT RIGHT THERE, SON!
BOOT

WHAT ARE YOU TALKING ABOUT?
BLINK

I OPPOSE THIS MARRIAGE!
melon
GLUK
HUH...?

RANMA ?
EH ?

JUST WHO DO YOU THINK I'M TRYING TO MARRY ?!
TO MARRY THAT WOMAN, YOU MUST DEFEAT ME FIRST!

YES.
PILL WEAR OFF ?

ME, DEARIE.

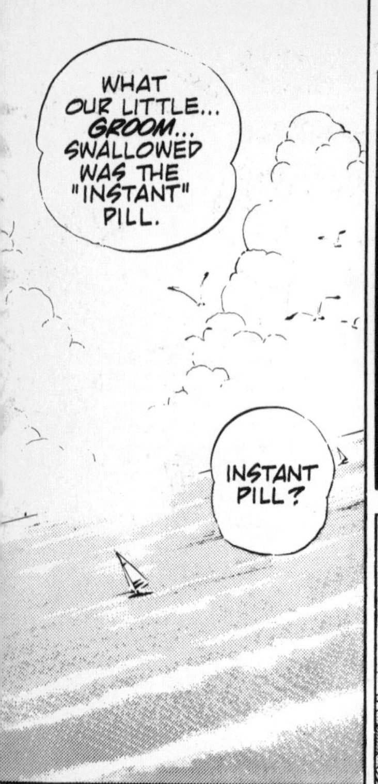
WHAT OUR LITTLE... *GROOM*... SWALLOWED WAS THE "INSTANT" PILL.
INSTANT PILL?

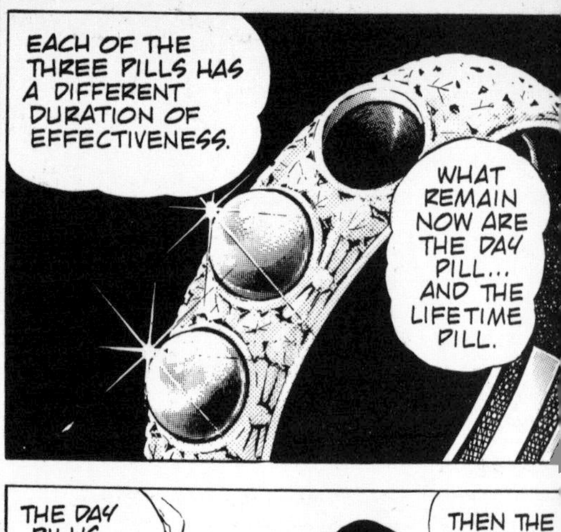
EACH OF THE THREE PILLS HAS A DIFFERENT DURATION OF EFFECTIVENESS.
WHAT REMAIN NOW ARE THE DAY PILL... AND THE LIFETIME PILL.
THE DAY PILL'S EFFECTS LAST ONE ENTIRE DAY...
THEN THE LIFETIME PILL LASTS...?

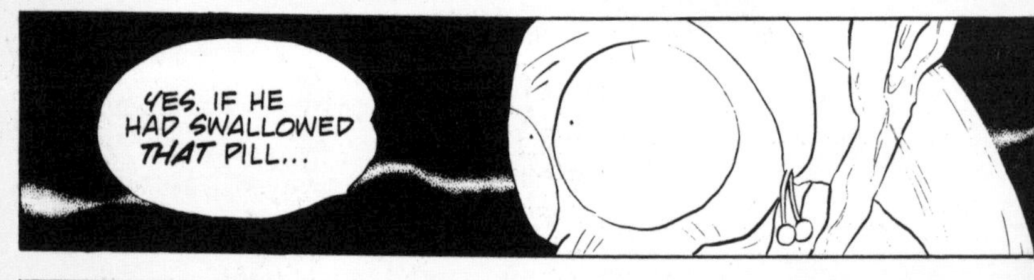
YES. IF HE HAD SWALLOWED *THAT* PILL...

I'D BE SENDING OUT INVITATIONS TO OUR WEDDING!
NYAHAHAHA!
THAT WAS CLOSE ONE, RANMA.
I DON'T THINK HE HEARS YOU...

BOOOON
TEE HEE HEE
WHEEE!
YOU DATE WITH SHAMPOO?
NOW WHICH GIRL SHALL I PICK?
BABUMP BABUMP
OH SHAMPOO!
HAPPY?
HYOI
TOP

CHIRRUP CHEEERUP-RUP-RUP

HONESTLY, RANMA.

INN

OOOHHH OOOHHH BOO HOO HOO

JUST GET OVER IT, WILL YOU?

TUP

IS PERFECT.

SHAMPOO?

I MAKE RANMA TAKE THIS WHILE HE SLEEP!
POP

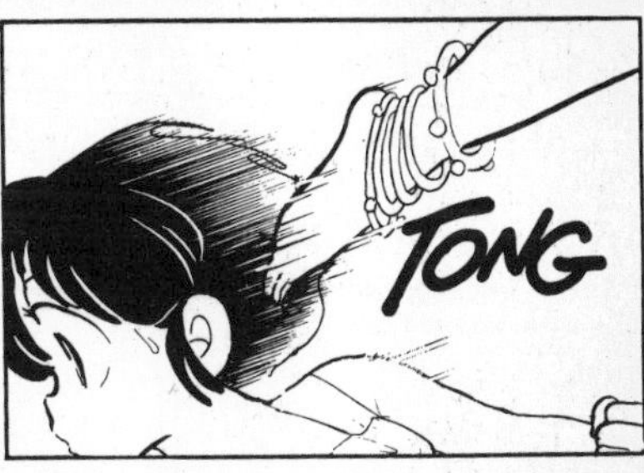
TONG

DON'T YOU EVER GIVE UP?!
WHSHHH

AAAKK!!
FLAP FLAP

ERG!
BOING

YOU FALL IN LOVE WITH SHAMPOO!
NOW, RANMA...
NGAAA
SNAG

HOW DO YOU LIKE THIS ?!
BLOOSH
BWAH!

IT DOESN'T WORK WHEN YOU'RE BOTH GIRLS!
WH-WHAT THE-- ?

FEH...
AFTER RANMA TAKE PILL...
FLIP

...I CHANGE RANMA BACK!
VIP
POIK
OW!
HAHAHA! YOU MISS--

--ED!
POP

GLMP
AIYAAA!
UH-OH!

Part 10
I WON'T FALL IN LOVE!

WHAT?! A LOVE PILL?! AKANE?!
CHIRRUP
CHIRRUP-RUP-RUP
INN

BUT AKANE...
DAD! WILL YOU STOP INTERFERING ?!
SPLASH
I NO THINK SO!
BOING
BWAH!
I'LL BE THE ONE TO CHOOSE WHO I LOOK...
POP
OH AKANE--!
INN
KABOOOM

TWINK!
THE ONLY PILLS LEFT WERE...

THE DAY PILL AND THE LIFETIME PILL. WHICH ONE DID YOU SWALLOW?
I DON'T KNOW...

WHAT HAPPENS IF SHE TOOK THE LIFETIME PILL?
POP
THE EFFECT WOULD LAST HER ENTIRE...

BIFF
BOOM
BAM
No peeking

HHSSSHHHH

...venirs
FLAP FLAP
CHILLED RAMEN
CAT CAFE
TANNING OIL
EH...?
COTS FOOD SHOWER

WHICH MEANS ?
NO NEED TO WORRY.
SHKK SHKK

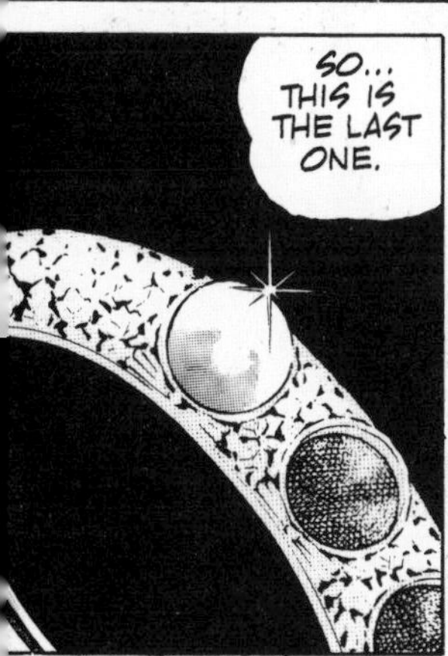

SO... THIS IS THE LAST ONE.

IS THAT ALL ?
REALLY ?!
WHAT YOU SWALLOWED WAS THE DAY PILL.
Phew
CHILLED RAMEN

IF IT'S ONLY THE DAY PILL, WHAT'S THERE TO GET ALL WORKED UP ABOUT?
WHAT D'YOU MEAN, "IS THAT ALL"?

JUST BECAUSE IT'S NOT YOUR PROBLEM...
TAPTAP
.....

HM?
No peeking
BEFORE YOU LOOK AT SOMETHING YOU DON'T WANT TO...
SHIMMER

HOW ABOUT YOU SETTLE FOR ME?

WHA...?

R-REALLY?
OF COURSE NOT, DUMMY!

PFOO!
TUG!
CHILLED RAMEN
MOOSH

I'M NOT GOING TO LET SOME PILL BEAT ME!
ALL I HAVE TO DO IS NOT LOOK AT ANY MEN FOR 24 HOURS!
AKANE!
TMP TMP

WAHAHAHA
YOU GO, GIRL!
OH SHUT UP!
OBBLE

BONG
OKAY. BUT WATCH OUT FOR THAT WALL.

LEAVE ME ALONE!

SKREEEK
WHOOPS! SILLY ME! SHE DID SWALLOW THE LIFETIME PILL!

...GO ON...
SHFF
I...I CAN'T...

N...NOW WHERE AM I...?

HUF HUF
FOOD
IRS
ICE

AKANE.. IF YOU ONLY KNEW...

SQUISH
TMP TMP

SQUORSH
UH...?

BOOOOM
A TINY BIT OF SYMPATHY WOULDN'T KILL YOU!
RANMA, YOU JERK!
VWIP
AKANE!
HM?
TM TM TM
SO WHAT IF I...
I'VE HAD ENOUGH!
TUG
BOOT
.....
AKA--

WHAT WAS THAT FOR!?
THERE'S A PIG DROWNING!
HUF HUF
BUKEEE!
P-CHAN, HOW DID YOU...?
AKANE, THE PILL YOU SWALLOWED...
ONE HUNDRED SWINGS!
BOOOOO
HIYAAA! HIYAAA! HIYAAA!
K-KUNO?!
KLUNK

.....
VORP
HUF HUF HUF HUF

YOU REALLY ARE JEALOUS!
DENY IT ALL YOU WANT, RANMA...

POOM

THE PILL YOU SWALLOWED...
LISTEN, AKANE!

WHY ARE YOU SO INTERESTED, HUH?!
LISTEN TO ME!

NYAAAAH!
VROOOOOM
HEY, HEY!

MY KNIGHT ON A WHITE HORSE MIGHT COME ALONG!
NO WAY!
PUT ON YOUR BLINDFOLD! IF YOU LOOK AT SOME STRANGE GUY...
HUH?
K-K-KLUMP
K-K-KLUMP
K-K-KLUMP
WHHN-N-N-N-NEEE
WHAT--?
AKANE! ♪
IS MORE LIKE NUT ON WHITE HORSE.
ACK!

HYAH
SHFF
DON'T LOOK, AKANE!
GLOMP
EEEK!
THWOP
I'LL RESCUE YOU, AKANE!
BURBLE URBLE
URBLE
RANMA, YOU TURN BACK TO BOY-TYPE AND FALL IN LOVE WITH SHAMPOO!
......
HAK HAK HAK HAK-
WAAAH!
B-KEEEE!

......

YOU BETTER APPRECIATE THIS, AKANE!

SOB

SOB

SOB

IF YOU LOOK AT THAT OLD FREAK...

BLORSH

YOUR WHOLE LIFE IS RUINED! SO...

...I'M CHANGING BACK INTO A GUY FOR YOU!

SOB

......

HCSHHH! HH! H!

......

UM...
HAVE YOU... FALLEN FOR ME?

RANMA...

...HOW **STUPID** WILL YOU GET BEFORE YOU **STOP**?!

B-BUT...THE PILL...YOU SWALLOWED IT, AND...

YES! AND THANKS TO YOU NEARLY DROWNING ME... HERE IT IS!

SPPT...

STUPID THING!

VISSHH

WHAT A WASTE!

BOOOOM

GLMP

......

I WAS TRYING TO TELL YOU THAT YOU TOOK THE LIFETIME PILL!

RANMA, YOU TAKE DAY PILL, YES?

OH MY. IS THAT YOUR NEW GIRLFRIEND?

I DID NOT!

SOB SOB SOB

BUT I'M NOT AN OCTOPUS!

THAT'S WHAT *YOU* SAY!

Part 11

ABDUCTION OF...AKANE?

I'VE BEEN WANTING THIS!

OINK

I'M HAPPY FOR YOU, AKANE.

HEH HEH HEH HEH HEH HEH

AKANE TENDO... BETROTHED OF RANMA SAOTOME...

HUH?

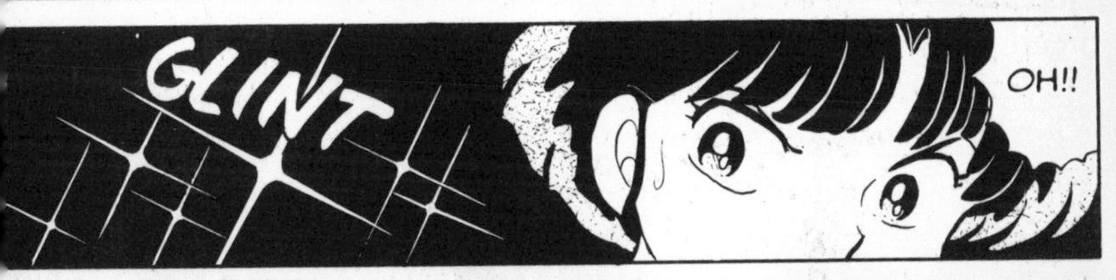

LOOK OUT!

SHH SHH

OH MY!

THOK

SHP
OINK..
SKWRK
NOW I'VE GOT YOU...
HEH HEH HEH HEH HEH
AND JUST WHO ARE YOU?!
OINK
OH, WHAT A STRANGE MAN.

SHHHH

PAP

YOU TELL RANMA SAOTOME...

THAT IF HE WANTS TO GET AKANE TENDO BACK...
OINK
HEY...

...HE MUST COME TO THE PLACE SHOWN ON THAT TICKET!
WAHAHAHAHA
OINK
B-BOING...
HEY, WAIT A MINUTE!

AKANE... HE THOUGHT THAT PIGGY WAS YOU!
HE'LL *PAY* FOR THAT!!
GRRRR

Shooting Gallery
50¢
YAH
HAHA
WHEE
NIHAO, RANMA!
HEY, SHAMPOO.
TINKLE
RANMA COME DATE WITH SHAMPOO!
SORRY, I GOTTA GO RESCUE AKANE.
IT'S NOT *ME!*
WHAT A MAROON, CALLIN' ME OUT TO A PLACE LIKE THIS...

PLEASE DO COME! THESE REAL CHINESE ACROBAT CIRCUS FROM CHINA!

CHINESE ACROBATS

WHEE

FAMILY FUN

YAY

WEIRD. I DON'T KNOW ANYBODY IN THE...

IT'S BEEN A LONG TIME, RANMA SAOTOME...

WHA--?

HEH HEH HEH HEH HEH

TONIGHT'S SHOW SHOULD BE VERY ENTERTAINING.
HEH HEH HEH HEH HEH
Y-YOU'RE--
AIYAAA! MOUSSE!
OINK
RANMA SAOTOME...
UNTIL I WIN BACK SHAMPOO FROM YOU...
I SHALL KEEP AKANE TENDO A HOSTAGE!
STOP SQUEEZING HER! YOU'RE MAKING HER CRY!
OINK
WHAP
DO TELL WHY YOU THINK THAT LOOKS LIKE AKANE TENDO.
MUSH

HE HAVE BAD EYESIGHT. LIKE ALWAYS.
AAAH! WHEN DID THIS HAPPEN?!
OINK
EH?
POP
GONNNNNG
YAAAAAAAY!
CLAP CLAP CLAP CLAP CLAP CLAP CLAP CLAP
TEEHEE HEE HEE HEE
WOW, THAT'S AMAZING!
WE LUCKY TO GET FREE TICKET!
CLAP CLAP CLAP CLAP

BAH.
LAUGH WHILE YOU CAN...
...UNTIL YOUR *DEATH*...
GLINT
RANMA SAOTOME!
CLAP CLAP CLAP CLAP CLAP CLAP
NOW WE NEEDING YOUR HELP!
CHNK CHNK
ONE MEMBER OF AUDIENCE, PLEASE COME STAGE!

HAH!
VRRRR
OKAY, WE HAVE VOLUNTEER NOW!
VVVIP
OOOH!
CLAP CLAP CLAP CLAP CLAP CLAP
TOK
KLAK
KLAK
NOW, WHAT IS FATE OF POOR CAPTURED GIRL!?
HUH?
DUM DE DUM DUM!

GLINT
!
TAK TAK TAK
YOW!!
TAK TAK TAK
OOOOOOO!
WHAT THE...?
AIYAA.
IS ENTRANCE OF OUR BIG STAR!
KLANK
HUF HUF HUF

YAAAAAY!!
WELCOME PLEASE MU MU-CHAN, THE DUCK!
TH-THIS AIN'T NO ORDINARY DUCK...
AND WHAT A DUCK!
UH-OH!
FWAP FWAP
KSSHHH

TAK TAK TAK TAK
YAAY!
THAT CHICK'S JUST AS GOOD AS THE DUCK!
TUK
WHY... YOU... WEB-FOOTED...
Ptui!!
FWAP
GEH!
hssss

KABOOM!

BOMBS...?!

POP POP POP POP POP POP

POP POP POP POP POP POP

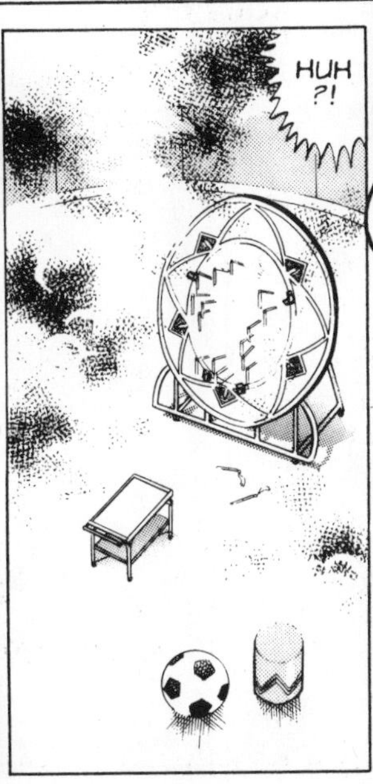

CLAP CLAP CLA CLAP CLAP CLAP CLAP CLAP CLAP CLAP CLAP CLAP
I THOUGHT SO! THAT DUCK WAS YOU!

HAK HAK
THOSE KNIVES WERE A MERE GREETING.
BAH...
CLATTER

I'LL MAKE SURE I ENJOY IT!
SINCE YOU WENT TO THE TROUBLE GIVING ME THIS TICKET...
KOFF
ADMIT ONE
CHINESE ACROBAT CIRCUS

PREPARE YOURSELF, RANMA SAOTOME!
THE CIRCUS FROM HELL IS JUST BEGINNING!

Part 12

DUCK, RANMA, DUCK!

HWOOOOOO
DO YOU KNOW...
GLUG
...WHAT THIS IS, RANMA?
WATER... ?

SEVERAL MONTHS AGO IN CHINA...
IT IS THE FRUIT OF MY LABORS!
IT IS NO ORDINARY WATER.
HERE SIR, IS LEGENDARY TRAINING GROUND OF CURSED SPRING, JUSENKYO.
SPSH SPSH
I SHALL TRAIN ATOP THESE BAMBOO POLES FOR THE DEFEAT OF RANMA SAOTOME!
FWIP
AIYAAA! YOU FALL IN YAHZU-NIICHUAN!
AND SO I TOOK MY FIRST GLORIOUS STEP TO VICTORY!
BLOOSH
GLORIOUS, HUH?

SPRING OF DROWNED DUCK HAVE TRAGIC STORY OF DUCK WHAT DROWN THERE 1300 YEAR AGO...
BURBL
BRBL
NOW, WHOEVER FALL IN SAME SPRING...

OH, GET REAL!
BOP BOP
EEK! EEK!
BITE ME, WILL YOU, RANMA!?

CHOMP

SO...
WHRRR...

SKRITCH SKRITCH SKRITCH

EH?
POP

HWOOOOOO
KLATTER

EYAAA!
SPLASH
YOU SAY THIS WATER IS THE FRUIT OF YOUR LABORS?

...FROM THE SPRING OF THE DROWNED DUCK!

WHAT THE--?

SHAMPOO...
KWAK
MOUSSE!
SHAMPOO NO LET YOU HURT RANMA!
VIP
SHAMPOO HAVE NO INTENTION OF DATE WITH YOU!
BAM
HUH ?
GRRRR

COME 'N GET ME!
FWAP
WHOA!
BOING
TAK
TAK TAK
WAPA
WHEE
HAHA
VROOOOM
TAK
TAK
SHH SHH

DOESN'T HE EVER RUN OUT ?!
FWAP
SHAA
EEP!
POP
POP
GOLDFISH

SPLAT
LOOK OUT!
PLISH PLOSH
GOLD FISH CATCH ¥50
LET'S TRY IT!
HEY! DUCK CATCHING!
QUAK QUAK QUAK
OH DEAR DEAR ME...
CHK CHK
HEY...
MOUSSE! WHY YOU--!

VRRR

I'VE HAD *ENOUGH* OF YOUR STUPID GRUDGE!

POIT

POIT

POIT

NOW SHAMPOO *MAD!*

BLOOSH

VROOM

YAAA AAH!!

MYOW! MYOW! MYOW!

.....

AKANE TENDO...
EEEEEK!

SHP!

BOOP

OHHHHHH..

THIS TIME I HAVE YOU FOR SURE!

BIG CHINESE ACROBATIC MAGIC SHOW START VERY SOON!

WHAT'S THIS? A GIRL THAT BECOMES A DUCK?

Amazing Duck Girl! THE REAL THING!

HEY, SHE'S CUTE.

WHIRRRRRR...

HUH?

NOOOOOOOM

AAAAARGH!

MOW! MOW!

RANMA SAOTOME...

IF YOU DO NOT COME TO HER RESCUE... YOUR FIANCÉE WILL SPEND HER LIFE PADDLING ON A POND!

YAAAY!!

YAAAY!

TO BE CONTINUED.

COMPLETE OUR SURVEY AND LET US KNOW WHAT YOU THINK!

☐ Please do NOT send me information about VIZ products, news and events, special offers, or other information.

☐ Please do NOT send me information from VIZ's trusted business partners.

Name: ______________________________

Address: ______________________________

City: ________________ **State:** ________ **Zip:** ____________

E-mail: ______________________________

☐ **Male** ☐ **Female** **Date of Birth (mm/dd/yyyy):** ___/___/_____ (**Under 13? Parental consent required**)

What race/ethnicity do you consider yourself? (please check one)

☐ Asian/Pacific Islander ☐ Black/African American ☐ Hispanic/Latino

☐ Native American/Alaskan Native ☐ White/Caucasian ☐ Other: ____________

What VIZ product did you purchase? (check all that apply and indicate title purchased)

☐ DVD/VHS ______________________________

☐ Graphic Novel ______________________________

☐ Magazines ______________________________

☐ Merchandise ______________________________

Reason for purchase: (check all that apply)

☐ Special offer ☐ Favorite title ☐ Gift

☐ Recommendation ☐ Other ______________________________

Where did you make your purchase? (please check one)

☐ Comic store ☐ Bookstore ☐ Mass/Grocery Store

☐ Newsstand ☐ Video/Video Game Store ☐ Other: ____________

☐ Online (site: ______________________________)

What other VIZ properties have you purchased/own? ______________________________

____

How many anime and/or manga titles have you purchased in the last year? How many were VIZ titles? **(please check one from each column)**

ANIME	MANGA	VIZ
☐ None	☐ None	☐ None
☐ 1-4	☐ 1-4	☐ 1-4
☐ 5-10	☐ 5-10	☐ 5-10
☐ 11+	☐ 11+	☐ 11+

I find the pricing of VIZ products to be: **(please check one)**

☐ Cheap ☐ Reasonable ☐ Expensive

What genre of manga and anime would you like to see from VIZ? **(please check two)**

☐ Adventure ☐ Comic Strip ☐ Science Fiction ☐ Fighting

☐ Horror ☐ Romance ☐ Fantasy ☐ Sports

What do you think of VIZ's new look?

☐ Love It ☐ It's OK ☐ Hate It ☐ Didn't Notice ☐ No Opinion

Which do you prefer? **(please check one)**

☐ Reading right-to-left

☐ Reading left-to-right

Which do you prefer? **(please check one)**

☐ Sound effects in English

☐ Sound effects in Japanese with English captions

☐ Sound effects in Japanese only with a glossary at the back

THANK YOU! Please send the completed form to:

NJW Research
42 Catharine St.
Poughkeepsie, NY 12601

All information provided will be used for internal purposes only. We promise not to sell or otherwise divulge your information.